VINTAGE BORN IN 1973 All ORIGINAL BOOK

Celebrating your year

1973

A memorable year for

Contents

Introduction: A Glimpse into 1973

Chapter 5: Fashion, and Popular Leisure Activities

Chapter 6: Technological Advancements and Popular Cars

Chapter 7: The Cost of Things

Chapter 8: Iconic Advertisements of 1973

Introduction
A Year to Remember - 1973
For Those Whose Hearts Belong to 1973

To our cherished readers who hold a special connection to the year 1973, whether it's because you were born in this remarkable year, celebrated a milestone, or hold dear memories from that time, this book is a tribute to you and your unique connection to an unforgettable era.

In the pages that follow, we invite you to embark on a captivating journey back to 1973, a year of profound historical significance. For those with a personal connection to this year, it holds a treasure trove of memories, stories, and experiences that shaped the world and touched your lives.

Throughout this book, we've woven together the tapestry of 1973, providing historical insights, personal stories, and interactive activities that allow you to relive and celebrate the significance of this special year.

As you turn the pages and immerse yourself in the events and culture of 1973, we hope you'll find moments of nostalgia, inspiration, and the opportunity to rekindle cherished memories of this extraordinary year.

This book is dedicated to you, our readers, who share a unique bond with 1973. May it bring you joy, enlightenment, and a deeper connection to the rich tapestry of history that weaves through your lives.

With warm regards,

EdwardArtLab.com

Chapter 1:
Politics and Leading Events around the World

1.1 The Global Stage in 1973: Where Were You?
Vietnam War Ceasefire on Jan 28th, 1973

On January 28, 1973, a significant moment in history occurred when a ceasefire was signed, officially ending the involvement of American ground troops in the Vietnam War.

Vietnam War 1973 | "Cease-fire" reads the headline of a news

This ceasefire marked the culmination of years of conflict that had deeply divided American society and had a profound impact on Vietnam. It was part of the broader Paris Peace Accords, which aimed to bring an end to the Vietnam War. As a result of the ceasefire, American combat troops were withdrawn from Vietnam, effectively bringing their direct military involvement to a close.

7

While the ceasefire brought a semblance of peace, it did not resolve all the issues surrounding the Vietnam War. The war continued for two more years between the North and South Vietnamese forces until the fall of Saigon in 1975. Nevertheless, the signing of the ceasefire on January 28, 1973, marked a pivotal moment in the conflict, and it remains a significant event in the history of both the United States and Vietnam.

03/29/1973 - U.S. withdraws from Vietnam

Phu Cuong, South Vietnam, 1973

Chilean Coup: Allende Ousted by Pinochet (Sept. 11, 1973)

On September 11, 1973, a significant event unfolded in Chilean history. Chile's Marxist president, Salvador Allende, was overthrown in a coup, and General Augusto Pinochet assumed power.

Smoke rises from La Moneda, the presidential palace, after it was bombed during a military coup on Sept. 11, 1973

Soldiers and firefighters carry President Salvador Allende's body out of the destroyed La Moneda presidential palace after the coup on Sept. 11, 1973

Salvador Allende had been democratically elected as Chile's president in 1970, representing a socialist government. However, his presidency faced significant challenges, including economic instability and political polarization. The coup, which had the support of the United States government, marked a tragic turning point. General Pinochet's regime was characterized by authoritarian rule, human rights abuses, and the suppression of political dissent. It resulted in a period of repression and violence that had a lasting impact on Chilean society.

General Pinochet

This event is a stark example of the complex political dynamics and foreign intervention that shaped Latin American history during the 20th century. The Pinochet era in Chile left a deep imprint on the nation's politics and society and is remembered as a dark chapter in its history.

Yom Kippur War (1973) and U.S.-Sponsored Cease-Fire Accord

The fourth and largest Arab-Israeli conflict erupted on October 6th as Egyptian and Syrian forces attacked Israel on the holiest day of the Jewish calendar, Yom Kippur. This conflict, known as the Yom Kippur War, was a pivotal moment in the ongoing Arab-Israeli conflicts.

Tensions in the region had been escalating for years, and the surprise attack on Yom Kippur caught Israel off guard. However, after weeks of intense fighting, a U.S.-sponsored cease-fire accord was signed between Egypt and Israel on November 11th.

The Yom Kippur War highlighted the volatility of the Middle East and the deep-rooted conflicts between Israel and its Arab neighbors. It led to significant political developments and diplomatic efforts in the region, including the Camp David Accords in 1978, which paved the way for Egypt to become the first Arab country to officially recognize Israel.

October 1973. Israeli soldiers

This conflict remains a critical chapter in the history of the Arab-Israeli disputes and their broader implications for regional stability and international diplomacy.

1.2 Leaders and Statesmen: Movers and Shakers of '73

Richard Nixon

Richard Nixon was elected the 37th President of the United States (1969-1974) after previously serving as a U.S. Representative and a U.S. Senator from California. After successfully ending American fighting in Vietnam and improving international relations with the U.S.S.R. and China, he became the only President to ever resign the office, as a result of the Watergate scandal.

Georges Pompidou (France):

Georges Pompidou served as the President of France and played a significant role in French politics and diplomacy during his tenure.

Georges Pompidou served as the President of France from 1969 until his passing in 1974. He was a pivotal figure in French politics during a period of domestic and international challenges. As president, Pompidou worked on modernizing France's economy and strengthening its international ties. His presidency also marked a period of improved relations between France and the United States. Unfortunately, Pompidou's time in office was cut short by his death in 1974, leading to the election of his successor, Valéry Giscard d'Estaing. Pompidou's leadership is remembered for its focus on economic development and his role in shaping France's position in the world during the early 1970s.

Leonid Brezhnev

In 1973, Leonid Brezhnev held the position of General Secretary of the Communist Party of the Soviet Union, making him the de facto leader of the Soviet Union. During that time, he wielded immense power and was indeed the most influential figure in the country. Brezhnev's leadership in 1973 played a crucial role in shaping Soviet foreign policy, particularly during the era of détente with the United States, as well as the domestic policies and direction of the Soviet Union during that period.

Activity
Historical Crossword - 1973

ACROSS

2. Date of the Chilean coup when Salvador Allende was overthrown

3. The political ideology of Salvador Allende in Chile

6. The capital city of Chile

7. Ceasefire agreement that ended U.S. involvement in the Vietnam War

8. The military leader who took power in Chile after the coup

9. Event on January 28, 1973, that marked the end of U.S. ground troops' involvement in the Vietnam War

10. The region where the Yom Kippur War mainly occurred

DOWN

1. The country where the Yom Kippur War took place

4. The month when the Yom Kippur War started

5. The U.S.-sponsored accord that helped end the Yom Kippur War

Chapter 2:
The Iconic Movies, TV Shows, and Awards

2.1 Hollywood's Finest: Memorable Films of '73
American Graffiti

The classic film "American Graffiti" premieres in the United States during August. The film was directed by George Lucas, who also co-wrote it with Gloria Katz and Willard Huyck. The coming-of-age comedy starred Richard Dreyfuss, Ron Howard, Cindy Williams, and Candy Clark. The film was praised by critics and earned five Academy Award nominations, four Golden Globe nominations, and two Golden Globe wins. "American Graffiti" was notable for its unique and innovative storytelling style, along with its nostalgic take on Sixties teen culture in California. In 1995, it was deemed an important cultural film and selected for preservation by the United States Library of Congress.

Serpico

Sidney Lumet's tense, scorching tale of one NYPD cop who dared to resist an entrenched culture of corruption was an ideal vehicle for the brooding Al Pacino, just one year after his "Godfather" triumph. The fact that "Serpico" was based on a recent true story only increased the film's impact.

Paper moon

In Peter Bogdanovich's sublime depression-era comedy, real-life father-daughter Ryan and Tatum O'Neal were small-time hustlers traveling the Midwest in search of suckers. The irresistible Tatum, just nine years old, won an Oscar, becoming the youngest recipient ever. The Oscar-nominated Madeleine Kahn was also exceptional playing exotic dancer Trixie Delight.

Day of the Jackal

Fred Zinnemann directed this taut thriller about a hired assassin (Edward Fox) whose target was French president Charles de Gaulle. The film featured vivid European locales and a top international cast, including Michael Lonsdale, Cyril Cusack, and many others. Zinnemann's assured direction and a lean, no-nonsense script kept the tension building to a breathtaking climax.

Mean Streets

Martin Scorsese's gritty breakthrough film tracked the fortunes of two cousins, Harvey Keitel and Robert De Niro, both small-time hoods in Little Italy. Keitel was superb, but De Niro really soared in the smaller but showier role of erratic Johnny Boy. This marked a turning point for the actor, who cemented his stardom the following year in "The Godfather, Part 2."

The last detail

Oscar-nominated Jack Nicholson played Billy Buddusky, a rough and rowdy career sailor assigned to transport fellow enlistee Meadows (Randy Quaid) to the stockade. Feeling sorry for the young prisoner, he and fellow escort Mulhall (Otis Young) resolved to show Meadows a good time on the way. Hal Ashby's salty drama made you glad you joined the party.

2.2: Small Screen Wonders: TV Shows That Captivated the Nation
Star Trek: The Animated Series (1973)

22 episodes of The Animated Series were aired between September 1973 and October 1974. Reruns continued on NBC through 1975. The series was produced by the experienced animation house Filmation and the episodes were scripted by professional science fiction and Star Trek writers, including Larry Niven, D.C. Fontana, David Gerrold, and Samuel A. Peeples.

Schoolhouse Rock! (1973)

Schoolhouse Rock — with its distinctive animation created by Phil Kimmelman and Associates and sweet, catchy songs penned by master songwriters like Bob Dorough and Lynn Ahrens — provided a healthy dose of quality "edutainment" for millions of American schoolchildren throughout the 1970s and early 1980s. Not only did the show help kids sharpen their skills in math, grammar and science, but it provided progressive lessons on civic and social topics

Kojak (1973)

Kojak was an American crime drama television series created by Abby Mann. It revolved around the efforts of the tough and incorruptible Lieutenant Theo Kojak, a bald, dapper New York City policeman who had a fondness for lollipops and often used the catchphrase, "Who loves ya, baby?".

The series aired in the USA on CBS from October 24, 1973, to March 18, 1978. It consisted of 121 hour-long episodes spread across five seasons.

2.3 The Red Carpet: Prestigious Film Awards and Honors
Oscar
Best Actor in a Leading Role

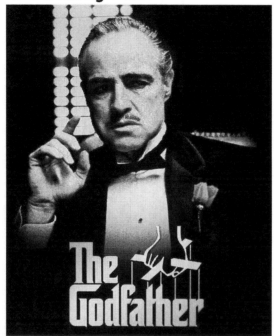

Marlon Brando

The Godfather

Brando's career went into decline in the 1960s, with expensive flops such as One-Eyed Jacks (1961), which he also directed, and Mutiny on the Bounty (1962). Aside from his preternatural talent, the actor had become notorious for his moodiness and demanding on-set behavior, as well as his tumultuous off-screen life. Francis Ford Coppola, the young director of The Godfather, had to fight to get him cast in the coveted role of Vito Corleone. Brando won the role only after undergoing a screen test and cutting his fee to $250,000–far less than what he had commanded a decade earlier. With one of the most memorable screen performances of all time, Brando rejuvenated his career, and The Godfather became an almost-immediate classic.

Best Actor in a Supporting Role

The 1972 film version of Cabaret won eight Academy Awards, one of which (for best supporting actor) went to Grey. He also earned a Golden Globe Award and the BAFTA Award for most promising newcomer for his performance.

Joel Grey, original name Joel David Katz, (born April 11, 1932, Cleveland, Ohio, U.S.), American actor, singer, and dancer who was best known for his riveting performance as the depraved and worldly master of ceremonies in the Kander and Ebb musical Cabaret, in both the 1966 stage version and the 1972 film adaptation.

Best Actress in a Leading Role

Liza Minnelli
Cabaret

Liza Minnelli, in full Liza May Minnelli, (born March 12, 1946, Hollywood, California, U.S.), American actress and singer perhaps best known for her role as Sally Bowles in Bob Fosse's classic musical film Cabaret (1972). In 1973 Liza won both the Academy Award for best actress for her role in Cabaret and an Emmy Award for her performance as the star of the previous TV season's spectacular Liza with a "Z".

Best Actress in a Supporting Role

Eileen Heckart won the Best Supporting Actress award at the 45th Academy Awards in 1973 for her performance in the movie "Butterflies are Free"1. She was presented with the award by Robert Duvall and Cloris Leachman1. Eileen Heckart was an American stage and screen actress, born on March 29, 1919, in Columbus, Ohio2

Activity
1973 Entertainment Trivia Quiz

Test your knowledge of entertainment in 1973 with this fun trivia quiz. See how many questions you can answer correctly!

Instructions:

Read each question carefully.

Choose the correct answer from the multiple-choice options.

Keep track of your score and see how well you did at the end.

Question 1:

Which classic film directed by George Lucas premiered in the United States in August 1973?

A) The Godfather

B) American Graffiti

C) Serpico

D) Paper Moon

Question 2:

Who won an Oscar for their role in "Paper Moon," becoming the youngest Oscar recipient ever at the age of nine?

A) Tatum O'Neal

B) Madeleine Kahn

C) Ryan O'Neal

D) Al Pacino

Question 3:

Which crime drama television series, featuring Lieutenant Theo Kojak, aired from 1973 to 1978?

A) Starsky & Hutch

B) Hawaii Five-O

C) Kojak

D) The Rockford Files

Question 4:

In 1973, which actor won the Academy Award for Best Actor in a Leading Role for his iconic performance in "The Godfather"?

A) Robert De Niro
B) Harvey Keitel
C) Al Pacino
D) Marlon Brando

Question 5:

Who received the Best Actress award at the 1973 Academy Awards for her role in "Cabaret"?

A) Julie Andrews
B) Barbra Streisand
C) Liza Minnelli
D) Audrey Hepburn
 aired from 1973 to 1978?

Question 6:

Which film earned Joel Grey an Oscar for Best Supporting Actor in 1973?

A) The Sting
B) The Exorcist
C) Chinatown
D) Cabaret

Question 7:

Eileen Heckart won the Best Supporting Actress award at the 1973 Academy Awards for her role in which movie?

A) Butch Cassidy and the Sundance Kid
B) Kramer vs. Kramer

C) Butterflies Are Free
D) The Graduate

Question 8:

How many episodes were there in "Star Trek: The Animated Series," which aired from 1973 to 1974?

A) 10 episodes
B) 16 episodes
C) 22 episodes
D) 30 episodes

Question 9:

Which educational and entertaining TV show provided lessons on math, grammar, and civic topics through catchy songs?

A) Sesame Street
B) Mr. Rogers' Neighborhood
C) Schoolhouse Rock!
D) The Electric Company

Question 10:

In "Serpico," who played the role of the NYPD cop who dared to resist corruption?

A) Al Pacino
B) Robert De Niro
C) Harvey Keitel
D) Marlon Brando

Scoring:

0-3 correct answers: You might need to brush up on your 1973 entertainment knowledge!

4-6 correct answers: Not bad! You know your classics.

7-9 correct answers: Impressive! You're a true entertainment buff.

10 correct answers: Wow, you're a 1973 entertainment expert!

Have fun testing your knowledge and reliving the entertainment highlights of 1973!

Chapter 3:
Music: Top Songs, Albums, and Awards

3.1 Musical Time Capsule: Chart-Toppers and Musical Trends

While all the political and cultural events of the late 60s and 70s had an impact on the music of 1973, the early seventies was a time when rock, pop, and soul, major musical styles of the day, had matured.

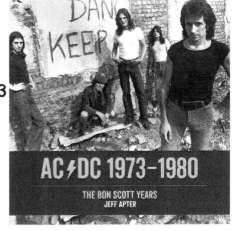

3.2 Renowned Bands of '73
The Bands of '73 Shaped
Classic Rock
AC/DC
Formation: Sydney,
Australia; November 1973

Formed in Australia by brothers Angus and Malcolm Young and company, AC/DC have basically defined hard rock. Propelled by an endless series of unmistakable riffs, the band has stomped their way to 200 million records sold worldwide, including 75 million in the U.S.

Key Tracks: Highway to Hell, Back in Black, You Shook Me All Night Long, Thunderstruck, Dirty Deeds Done Dirt Cheap

Bachman-Turner Overdrive

Formation: Thunder Bay, Ontario, Canada; 1973

Randy Bachman had hard rock success with The Guess Who, laying down lead guitar on tracks like "American Woman." But he decided to split with the band and eventually started working with his brothers Robbie (drums) and Tim (guitar), as well as Fred Turner (bass-vocals). Picking up "Overdrive" from the cover of a trucking magazine and tacking it on their last names, the band had a title, as well as an easy abbreviation: BTO.

Key Tracks: Let It Ride, Takin' Care of Business, You Ain't Seen Nothing Yet, Roll On Down the Highway, Hey You

Bad Company
Formation: Albury, Surrey, England; 1973

By the 1970s, rock had been around long enough that "supergroups" assembled by members of previously successful bands became a much bigger presence. The original lineup of Bad Company featured Mick Ralphs (former Mott the Hoople guitarist), Boz Burrell (former King Crimson bassist), and two former members of Free: drummer Simon Kirke and vocalist Paul Rodgers. The band was a smash in the U.S. and their native U.K. Rodgers in particular has frequently been cited as one of the greatest rock singers of all time, with his influence noted by everyone from Freddie Mercury to John Mellencamp, who referred to him as "the best rock singer ever" in a 1991 interview with Spin.

Key Tracks: Can't Get Enough, Movin' On, Feel Like Makin' Love, Rock 'n' Roll Fantasy

Cheap Trick
Formation: Rockford, Illinois; August 1973

The combo of guitarist Rick Nielsen, bassist Tom Petersson, and drummer Bun E. Carlos had played together as early as 1967, but they didn't form Cheap Trick until 1973. The original lead singer, Randy "Xeno" Hogan, didn't last long; he was replaced a few months later by the artist who would become the group's iconic frontman, Robin Zander. Regarded as the founders of "power pop," Cheap Trick combines rock fundamentals with insanely catchy tunes that still resonate.

Key Tracks: I Want You to Want Me, Dream Police, Surrender, If You Want My Love, The Flame

3.3 Notable Albums and Song Releases
Notable Albums
Quadrophenia

The Who, while outdone again by Pink Floyd and Led Zeppelin, put out one of their best albums in 1973, Quadrophenic It's a rock concept album, and one of the best. "The Real Me" features some of the finest drumming by Keith Moon on any Who track, and it features hits like "Love Reign O'e Me" and "I'm One".

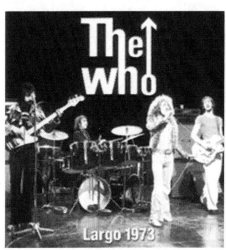 

Billion Dollar Babies

Alice Cooper's best album, Billion Dollar Babies, was also released in 1973. With hit songs like "Elected" and "No More Mister Nice Guy", Cooper wedged his place into rock stardom. There is not one weak song on the album; I recommend this album to all rock fans. In fact, I argue that this album is one of the best rock albums of all time.

Raw Power

Iggy Pop's Raw Power also came out in 1973, and while not the best of the year, the album was a break from the heavy mental and introduction of power pop that foreshadowed groups such as The Ramones. Iggy Pop was part of the Detroit grunge scene along with MC5.

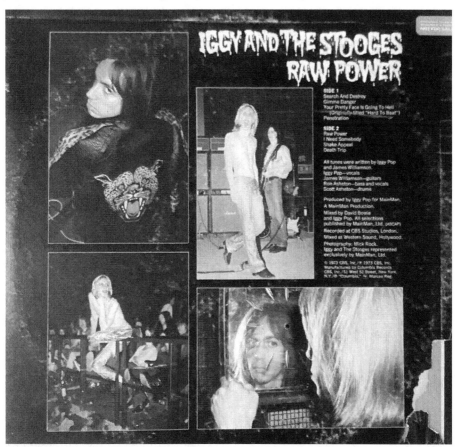

5 Best Songs From 1973
- Tie A Yellow Ribbon Round The Ole Oak Tree – Tony Orlando And Dawn
- Bad, Bad Leroy Brown – Jim Croce
- Killing Me Softly With His Song – Roberta Flack
- Let's Get It On – Marvin Gaye
- My Love – Paul McCartney & Wings

3.4 Recognizing Excellence: Music Awards and Honors

Grammy

Album of the Year

George Harrison

George Harrison (artist/producer), Ravi Shankar (artist), Bob Dylan (artist), Leon Russell (artist), Ringo Starr (artist), Billy Preston (artist), Eric Clapton (artist), Klaus Voormann (artist), Phil Spector (producer)
For "The Concert For Bangla Desh"

Best Album Notes

Tom T. Hall

Tom T. Hall (artist/album notes writer)
For "Tom T. Hall's Greatest Hits"

Best Chamber Music Performance
Julian Bream
Julian Bream
(artist), John
Williams (artist)
For "Julian And John
(Works By Lawes,
Carulli, Albeniz,
Granados)"

Best Classical Vocal Soloist Performance

Dietrich Fischer-Dieskau

For "Brahms: Die Schone Magelone"

Activity: Music Lyrics Challenge - Guess the Song Lyrics from '73

the answers to the "1973 Entertainment Trivia Quiz":

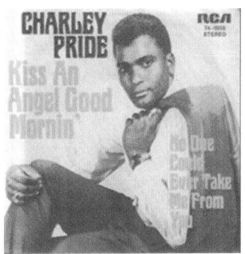

Best Country Song

Ben Peters

Ben Peters (songwriter)

For "Kiss An Angel Good Mornin'" artist: Charley Pride

Activity:
"Lyric Challenge - Guess the Song"

Introduction:
Step back in time to 1973 and test your knowledge of iconic songs from that year. In this activity, we'll focus on the classic hit "Killing Me Softly With His Song." L

Instructions:
Listen to the Song: Start by listening to the song "Killing Me Softly With His Song" by Roberta Flack. You can easily find it online or on your favorite music streaming platform.
Read the Partial Lyrics: We've provided a section of the song's lyrics with some words missing. Your task is to fill in the blanks with the correct missing words.

Strumming my _____ with his fingers (one time, one time)
Singing my _____ with his words (two times, two times)
Killing me softly with his song
Killing me softly with his song
Telling my _____ life with his words
Killing me softly with his song
I felt all _____ with fever, _____ by the crowd
I felt he'd found my _____ and read each one out loud
I prayed that he would _____, but he just kept right on

Share Your Results: Share your success with friends or family and see if they can guess the missing words too. It's a fun way to relive the music of 1973!

Chapter 4:
Sports in 1973

4.1 Sporting Achievements and Memorable Victories

John Newcombe became a five time grand slam winner taking the Australian Open. He also won the US Open that year. Ilie Năstase won the French Open for his second and final slam title, while Jan Kodeš took the Wimbledon for his third career title.

In women's tennis, **Margaret Court**, who has the highest number of grand slams till this date including pre-open era tennis, won the three grand slams, for a career total of 24 grand slam titles. The Wimbledon that Margaret missed out on was taken by Billie Jean King who also had a successful career with 12 slam titles.

Jack Nicklaus won his 12th major at the PGA Championship. He would go on to win six more in the following years for a total of 18 majors which stands for over three decades as the most major wins.

The heavyweight championship fight was conducted in Japan for the very first time and it was between two superstars. **George Foreman** easily emerged out as the winner against **Joe Frazier** in just two rounds.

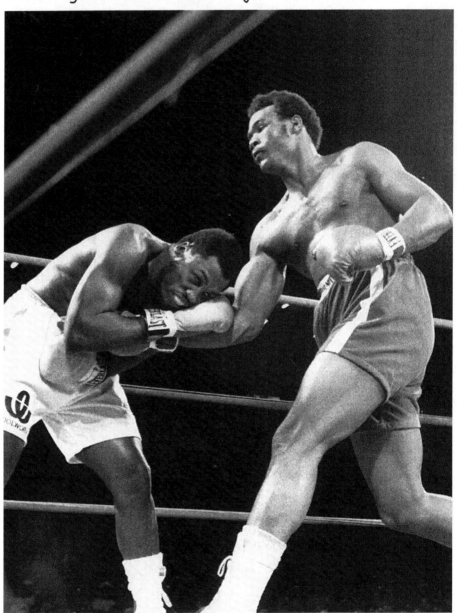

Below is a timeline of some significant results in the world of sport for the year 1973.

Date	Results
Jan	Tennis Australia Open won by John Newcombe and Margaret Court
Feb	Super Bowl held in Los Angeles won by Miami
April	Golf Masters won by Tommy Aaron
May	Tennis French Open won by Ilie Nastase and Margaret Court
June	Golf US Open won by Johnny Miller
July	The Cycling Tour de France won by Luis Ocaña
July	Tennis Wimbledon won by Jan Kodes and Billie Jean King
July	Golf The Open Championship won by Tom Weiskopf
Aug	Golf US PGA won by Jack Nicklaus (3)
Sep	Tennis US Open won by John Newcombe and Margaret Court
Oct	The Baseball World Series won by Oakland Athletics

4.2 American Sports: Champions and Championship Moments

NFL Pro Bowl

On January 21, 1973, the 23rd NFL Pro Bowl took place at Texas Stadium in Irving, Texas. In an exciting matchup, the American Football Conference (AFC) emerged victorious, defeating the National Football Conference (NFC) with a final score of 33-28. The game showcased the talent of some of the NFL's finest players.

The Most Valuable Player (MVP) of this thrilling Pro Bowl was O.J. Simpson, the outstanding running back from the Buffalo Bills. Simpson's exceptional performance on the field undoubtedly contributed significantly to the AFC's victory, earning him the prestigious MVP title for the game. Simpson's remarkable skills and contributions made him a standout player during this memorable Pro Bowl event

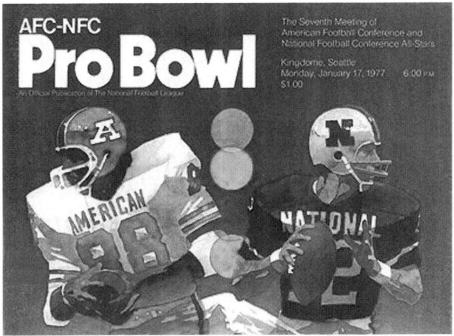

AFC-NFC Pro Bowl

THE THIRD ANNUAL MEETING OF AMERICAN FOOTBALL CONFERENCE AND NATIONAL FOOTBALL CONFERENCE ALL-STARS

Sunday, January 21, 1973, 3 p.m.
Texas Stadium
$1.00

Major League Baseball

In the 1973 World Series, the Oakland Athletics emerged as the champions of Major League Baseball (MLB). Here are the key details about their championship: The 1973 World Series was a best-of-seven showdown between the Oakland Athletics from the American League (AL) and the New York Mets from the National League (NL).

The A's, under the leadership of manager Dick Williams, showcased their talent with standout players like Reggie Jackson, Catfish Hunter, and Rollie Fingers.

The series took place from October 13 to October 21, 1973, with both teams vying for the championship.

The A's clinched the World Series title by winning four of the seven games.

Reggie Jackson, the star outfielder for the A's, was named the World Series Most Valuable Player (MVP) for his outstanding contributions during the championship.

Notable moments from the series included a thrilling Game 7, where the A's secured a 5-2 victory to seal the championship.

This victory marked the second consecutive World Series win for the Oakland Athletics, establishing them as a dominant force in MLB during the early 1970s.

4.3 Highlights from British Sports

1973 Rothmans International Tennis Tournament

The 1973 Rothmans International Tennis Tournament was a men's professional tennis tournament held on indoor carpet courts in the Royal Albert Hall in London, England. It was the third edition of the tournament and was held from 18-27 January 1973. The event was part of the 1973 World Championship Tennis circuit. Brian Fairlie won the singles title.

1973 Men of the Midlands

The 1973 Men of the Midlands was a professional invitational snooker tournament, that took place in January and February 1973 The tournament was won by Alex Higgins, who defeated Ray Reardon 5-3 in the final.

1972–73 British Ice Hockey season

The 1972–73 British Ice Hockey season featured the Northern League for teams from Scotland and the north of England and the Southern League for teams from the rest of England

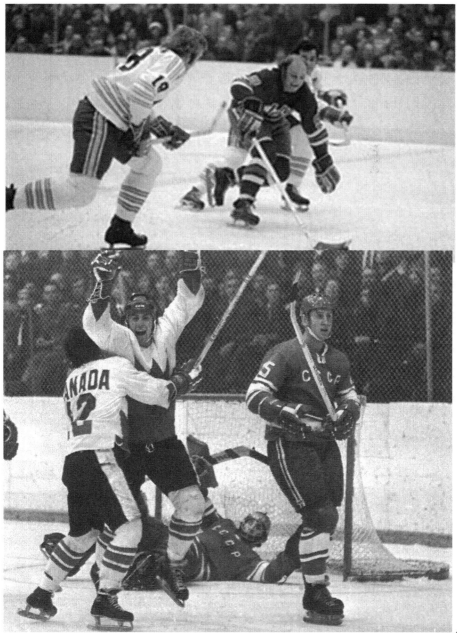

Activity:
Sports Trivia – Test Your Knowledge of 1973 Sports History

Welcome to a fun and engaging sports trivia activity that will test your knowledge of the sporting highlights of the year 1973. Let's see how much you remember about the champions, memorable moments, and significant events in various sports during that year.

Instructions:

Read the provided information about major sports events and champions in 1973.

Answer the trivia questions based on the information provided.

Trivia Questions:

1.Who won the Australian Open in men's tennis in 1973, becoming a five-time Grand Slam winner that year?

a) Roger Federer

b) Rafael Nadal

c) John Newcombe

d) Pete Sampras

2.Margaret Court, a legendary figure in women's tennis, won three Grand Slam titles in 1973. How many Grand Slam titles did she have in her entire career, including the pre-Open era?

a) 10

b) 15

c) 24

d) 30

3.Jack Nicklaus secured his 12th major victory at the PGA Championship in 1973. How many major championships did he ultimately win in his career?
a) 8
b) 12
c) 18
d) 24

4.In which country was the heavyweight championship fight between George Foreman and Joe Frazier held in 1973, marking the first time it took place there?
a) United States
b) Mexico
c) Japan
d) England

5.Who was named the Most Valuable Player (MVP) of the 23rd NFL Pro Bowl in 1973, where the AFC defeated the NFC?
a) Joe Namath
b) Johnny Unitas
c) O.J. Simpson
d) Jerry Rice

6.In the 1973 World Series, which team emerged as the champions of Major League Baseball?
a) New York Yankees
b) Oakland Athletics
c) Los Angeles Dodgers
d) Chicago Cubs

7.The 1973 Rothmans International Tennis Tournament was held in which city?
a) Paris
b) New York
c) London
d) Sydney
Who won the 1973 Men of the Midlands snooker tournament by defeating Ray Reardon in the final?
a) Alex Higgins
b) Ronnie O'Sullivan
c) Steve Davis
d) Mark Selby
Which British ice hockey season featured the Northern League for teams from Scotland and the north of England in 1973?
a) 1970-71
b) 1972-73
c) 1975-76
d) 1978-79

Chapter 5:

Pop Culture, Fashion, and Popular Leisure Activities

5.1 Fashion Flashback: What the World Wore in '73
Vintage 1973 Fashion including Shirts, Dresses, Suits and Coats
Fashion Clothing From the year 1973 including prices, descriptions and pictures inc. Shamrock and White Stripe Outfit, Polka Dot Sport Shirt, Wool Dress, Two Piece Ban-Lon Dress The prices shown for these Fashion Clothing are the price they were sold for in 1973 not today

Argyle Pullover 1973
Price: $18.00
Description Argyle pullover by Ram in Orlon acrylic. Choose from predominantly green, red or black.

Cashmere Tartan Sport Coat 1973
Price: $170.00
Description This cashmere tartan sport coat is great for holiday get-togethers and goes well with slacks.

Checked Sport Coat and Polyester Slacks 1973

Price: $22.00 (slacks) - $100.00 (sport coat)

Description Jaunty checked sport coat of polyester and nylon is a two button style with center vent and white polyester slacks

Double Breasted Wool Coat 1973

Price: $100.00

Description Dashing double breasted coat by Zero King cuts a fine figure in brown plaid wool with epaulets and warm alpaca wool collar. Wool/polyester lining.

Double Knit Wool Suit 1973

Price: $145.00

Description Stitched tucks distinguish a double-knit wool suit by Kimberly. With it, a long-sleeve polyester jacquard shirt, tie belted. Azure heather or beige.

Hadley Cardigan and Skirt 1973
Price: $36.00 - $60.00
Description This Hadley cashmere cable knit cardigan ($60.00) and shell ($44.00) in a light blue color go well with the Hadley tweed wrap-around skirt of wool/rayon/acetate for $36.00.

Happy Plaid Rain Coat 1973
Price: $65.00
Description Happy plaid multicolor raincoat and kerchief. Rayon/acetate with Zepel finish sheds rain and stain.

Paisley Slacks and Sport Coat 1973
Price: $23.50 - $90.00
Description Sport coat by Izod Ltd. of easy upkeep textured polyester with brass buttons in white. Slacks by Izod Ltd. in neat paisley print on navy, made of Avril rayon/cotton.

Houndstooth Cardigan 1973
Price: $30.00
Description This houndstooth acrylic cardigan by Damon comes in black, burgundy or brown all with natural color accents.

5.2 Leisure Pursuits: Entertainment and Hobbies

The year 1973 was marked by a variety of entertainment and hobbies that captivated people's leisure time. Here are some notable trends and pastimes from that era

1. Video Games:

The video game industry was in its infancy in 1973. One notable milestone was the release of "Pong" by Atari, which is often considered one of the earliest arcade video games.

2. Outdoor Activities:

Hiking, camping, and outdoor activities gained popularity in the 1970s as people sought to reconnect with nature. The environmental movement also gained momentum during this time.

3. Board Games:

Board games like "Monopoly," "Scrabble," and "Risk" continued to be popular choices for family entertainment.

4. Collectibles:

Collecting hobbies, such as coin collecting and stamp collecting, remained popular pastimes. Many people also collected vintage toys and memorabilia.

5. Books:

Bestselling books of 1973 included "Gravity's Rainbow" by Thomas Pynchon and "Fear of Flying" by Erica Jong, both of which sparked literary discussions.

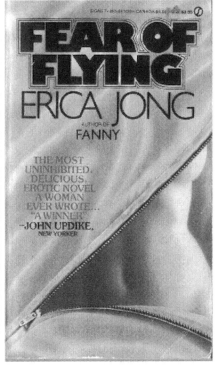

6. Sports and Recreation:

Sports like tennis, golf, and cycling were enjoyed as both hobbies and spectator events. The 1973 Wimbledon Championships and Tour de France were highly anticipated events.

7. Arts and Crafts:

The do-it-yourself (DIY) trend gained momentum, with people enjoying activities like knitting, crocheting, and making homemade crafts

8. Disco Dance:

The disco dance craze began to gain popularity in the early 1970s, with discotheques becoming hotspots for dance and socializing.

9. Home Entertainment:

The introduction of color television sets and improvements in home audio systems allowed families to enjoy entertainment from the comfort of their homes

10. Concerts and Live Performances:

Attending live concerts and performances by famous artists and bands was a cherished leisure activity, with music festivals drawing large crowds.

Led Zeppelin North American Tour 1973

Led Zeppelin's 1973 North American Tour was the ninth concert tour of North America by the English rock band. The tour was divided into two legs, with performances commencing on 4 May and concluding on 29 July 1973. Rehearsals took place at Old Street Film Studios in London.

Activity:
Fashion Design Coloring Page – Create Your '73-Inspired Outfit

Chapter 6:
Technological Advancements and Popular Cars

6.1 Innovations That Shaped the Future

1. Skylab, the United States' first space station, is launched

2. Concorde cuts flying time across the Atlantic in half flying at average speed of 954 mph

3.The Sears Tower opens in Chicago

4. Genetic Engineering USA by S Cohen and H Boyer

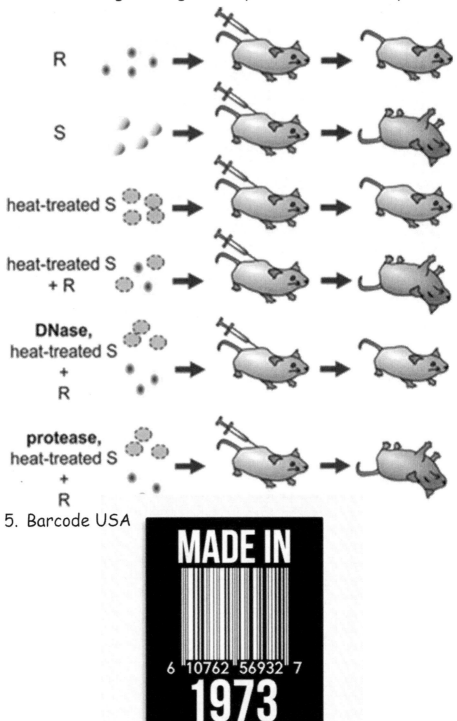

R

S

heat-treated S

heat-treated S + R

DNase, heat-treated S + R

protease, heat-treated S + R

5. Barcode USA

MADE IN

6 10762 56932 7

1973

6. Space Station USA Skylab

7. Jetski or Personal Watercraft USA Clayton Jacobson II (Original was only stand up and difficult to stay on) manufactured by Kawasaki

6.2 Cruisin' in Style: The Automobiles of '73
The 10 Fastest Cars of 1973
1. DeTomaso Pantera: 6.0 Seconds

Body Type Tested: Coupe
Engine: 351-cubic-inch V8
Horsepower: 266

Transmission:
5-speed manual
Axle Ratio: 3.50:1
Curb Weight: 2860

2. Porsche 911: 6.8 Seconds

Body Type Tested: Coupe
Engine: 143-cubic-inch flat six
Horsepower: 157

Transmission:
4-speed manual
Axle Ratio: 4.43:1
Curb Weight: 2485

3. Chevrolet Corvette

8.0 Seconds
1973 Chevrolet Corvette
Body Type Tested: Coupe
Engine: 350-cubic-inch V8

Horsepower: 275
Transmission:
3-speed automatic
Axle Ratio: 3.36:1
Curb Weight: 3416

4. Datsun 240Z: 8.8 Seconds

1973 Datsun 240Z
Body Type Tested: Coupe
Engine: 146-cubic-inch six
Horsepower: 151
Transmission: 4-speed manual
Axle Ratio: 3.90:1
Curb Weight: 2266

5. Dodge Charger: 10.0 Seconds
1973 Dodge Charger
Body Type Tested: Coupe
Engine: 400-cubic-inch V8
Horsepower: 175
Transmission: 3-speed automatic
Axle Ratio: 3.23:1
Curb Weight: 3550

6. Dodge Dart: 10.0 Seconds
1973 Dodge Dart Sport
Body Type Tested: Coupe
Engine: 340-cubic-inch V8
Horsepower: 240
Transmission: 3-speed automatic
Axle Ratio: 3.23:1
Curb Weight: 2985

7. Chevrolet Nova: 10.7 Seconds

1973 Chevrolet Nova
Body Type Tested: Sedan
Engine: 350-cubic-inch V8
Horsepower: 165
Transmission: 3-speed automatic
Axle Ratio: 3.08:1
Curb Weight: 3169

8. Mercury Capri: 10.7 Seconds

1973 Mercury Capri
Body Type Tested: Coupe
Engine: 155-cubic-inch V6
Horsepower: 107
Transmission: 4-speed manual
Axle Ratio: 3.22:1
Curb Weight: 2245

9. AMC Matador: 10.8 Seconds
1973 AMC Matador
Body Type Tested: Sedan
Engine: 401-cubic-inch V8
Horsepower: 255
Transmission: 3-speed automatic
Axle Ratio: 2.87:1
Curb Weight: 3250

10. Fiat 124 Sport Coupe: 10.8 Seconds
1973 Fiat 124 Sport Coupe
Body Type Tested: Coupe
Engine: 98-cubic-inch four
Horsepower: 90
Transmission: 5-speed manual
Axle Ratio: 4.13:1
Curb Weight: 2204

Activity

Wordsearch

Words to find:

Porsche   Charger   Capri
Corvette   Dart   Matador
Datsun   Nova   Fiat

```
A  J  C  W  R  D  N  V  Q  N  B  P  P  W  N  C  L  C  V  T
I  K  A  W  E  D  M  Q  R  U  M  Q  W  E  X  Y  W  Y  A  P
D  N  P  X  Q  G  W  N  H  Z  C  H  A  R  G  E  R  H  K  F
F  L  R  T  A  E  W  I  G  D  D  L  P  I  Z  P  Y  T  Q  O
C  M  I  T  G  K  Z  O  Q  R  A  I  J  J  A  N  B  B  X  C
U  O  W  T  Q  Z  H  F  Z  D  T  X  F  A  Q  K  R  W  V  S
L  F  K  X  R  S  G  J  J  S  S  E  W  A  B  A  A  F  W  P
P  O  R  S  C  H  E  N  W  Q  U  Q  S  C  X  B  P  W  Z  E
F  J  G  T  F  B  J  D  J  I  N  Q  Y  E  D  I  R  R  C  E
Y  O  I  J  V  E  H  A  N  K  C  H  R  J  S  X  A  Q  C  X
K  Y  L  U  F  I  U  R  N  F  Y  E  E  C  O  F  F  L  B  M
J  M  D  K  G  G  F  T  O  E  T  Q  U  D  P  U  I  R  K  A
X  O  M  X  X  M  J  M  E  X  T  V  Z  A  K  I  A  F  L  T
X  P  F  C  D  B  T  R  A  Z  B  C  F  Y  Y  D  T  H  U  A
D  I  E  R  U  H  R  R  U  S  X  G  D  Q  P  R  C  V  A  D
G  T  V  A  C  X  T  F  B  U  C  O  R  V  E  T  T  E  U  O
C  Z  L  K  N  Z  D  Z  J  R  O  U  C  B  Q  Z  D  D  N  R
D  J  Z  P  M  G  N  Y  R  P  G  U  Y  Y  P  W  S  W  O  B
P  U  B  C  K  F  W  E  N  O  V  A  F  W  E  Y  C  H  G  N
J  Z  K  L  O  P  W  M  A  F  X  C  D  I  Y  P  O  Z  K  G
```

Chapter 7: The Cost of Things

The Price Tag: Cost of Living in 1973

1973 COST OF LIVING

New House:	$32,500
Median Income:	$12,900
New Car:	$7,200
Minimum Wage:	$1.60/hour
Movie Ticket:	$2.69
Gasoline:	40 cents/gallon
Postage Stamp:	8 cents
Sugar:	49 cents/5 lbs
Milk:	$1.31/gallon
Coffee:	87 cents/pound
Eggs:	45 cents/dozen
Bread:	29 cents

THIS WEEK'S
BEST BUYS

PRICES SLASHED ON NEW & USED CARS

USED CARS

'69 CHEVY MALIBU SUPER SPORT
Automatic, Air Conditioning **$1495**

'67 MUSTANG
Gold, 3 speed, Air Conditioning **$1095**

'72 DODGE DEMON
Automatic, Air Conditioning
Vinyl Top **$1995**

'72 CHEVY IMPALA CONV
Automatic, Air Conditioning **$2595**

'70 PONTIAC GTO
Silver, 4 speed **$1395**

'73 CHEVY NOVA HATCHBACK
Silver, Air Conditioning ... **$2995**

NEW 1973 LEMANS
2 Dr., Ht.,
Auto, Power, Air **$3395**

NEW 1974 GRAND PRIX DEMO
Full Power, Air, List $6584
Electric Sun Roof **$5184**

NEW 1973 CATALINA DEMO
Automatic, Power Steering,
4 Dr. Sedan, Air, Vinyl Top **$2899**

NEW 1974 VENTURA HATCHBACK
Auto, Radio,
Air Conditioning **$3399**

100% FINANCING—ON THE SPOT DELIVERY

GUARANTEED RECONDITIONING AND INSPECTION!	GM USED CAR WARRANTY GOOD FOR TWO FULL YEARS
	NO MILEAGE LIMITATION

CURT W. BROWN
President

WILLIAM "BILL" BROWN

C. BROWN
PONTIAC PLACE
(Formerly Miller Pontiac)

4200 MAIN STREET
KANSAS CITY, MO.

NEW CARS **531-4200**   USED CARS **531-3133**

NEW! USED CAR LOT at HIGHWAY 50 & ELMWOOD
Hours: Mon. through Thurs. 'til 9 p.m.; Fri. and Sat. 'til 6 p.m.

Car prices 1973

1973 Grocery Prices

Poster points to huge food price increases: 1973

TIME

FOOD PRICES:
The Big Beef

Activity:
1973 Shopping List Challenge

Step back in time and experience the cost of living in 1973 by taking on the "1973 Shopping List Challenge." This interactive activity allows you to create your own shopping list and calculate the total cost based on the prices from that era. Get ready to explore the past and discover how much everyday items used to cost!

Groceries:

Bread (2 loaves): $0.50 - $0.60
Milk (1 gallon): $1.25 - $1.50
Eggs (1 dozen): $0.45 - $0.55
Ground beef (2 lbs): $1.00 - $1.25 per pound
Cereal (Corn Flakes): $0.60 - $0.70 per box
Coffee (Folgers, 1 lb): $1.50 - $1.75
Sugar (5 lbs): $0.50 - $0.60
Flour (5 lbs): $0.50 - $0.60
Butter (1 lb): $0.75 - $0.90
Fresh fruits (apples, oranges, bananas): Varies by type and season
Frozen TV dinners: $0.75 - $1.00 each
Canned soup (Campbell's): $0.25 - $0.35 per can
Soda (Coca-Cola, 6-pack): $0.60 - $0.75
Household Items:
Laundry detergent (Tide, 32 oz): $0.75 - $0.90
Dishwashing liquid (Joy, 16 oz): $0.40 - $0.50
Toilet paper (4-pack): $0.30 - $0.40
Paper towels (2 rolls): $0.40 - $0.50
Cleaning supplies(broom, mop, scrub brushes): Prices vary
Trash bags (box of 20): $0.75 - $0.90
Light bulbs (4-pack): $0.50 - $0.60
Batteries (AA, 4-pack): $0.50 - $0.60
Aluminum foil (25 sq ft): $0.40 - $0.50
Plastic wrap (100 ft): $0.50 - $0.60

Shopping List

- [ ] --
- [ ] --
- [ ] --
- [ ] --
- [ ] --
- [ ] --
- [ ] --
- [ ] --
- [ ] --
- [ ] --
- [ ] --

8.1 Marketing Masterpieces:Remembering Vintage Ads

Gosh, Yes - Vintage Ads! - The Clorox Co, 1973

1973 Ad for Marlboro Cigarettes retro Tobacco Cowboy

One good banana

deserves another.

Puma Bananas from Beconta.

Underwear bomb, 1973

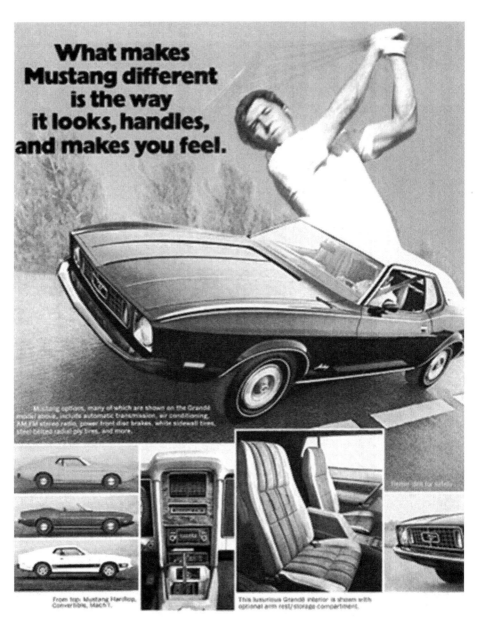

What makes Mustang different is the way it looks, handles, and makes you feel.

Mustang options, many of which are shown on the Grandé model above, include automatic transmission, air conditioning, AM/FM stereo radio, power front disc brakes, white sidewall tires, steel belted radial ply tires, and more.

From top: Mustang Hardtop, Convertible, Mach I.

This luxurious Grandé interior is shown with optional arm rest/storage compartment.

There are at least three reasons why Ford Mustang has been the top-selling car in its class since 1965.

Good looks. Mustang is sporty and sleek. Inside and out. Your choice of five models: Mach I, SportsRoof, Grandé, Hardtop and Convertible.

Good handling. Mustang's low silhouette and compact size make its handling as beautiful as its looks. You get independent front suspension with anti-sway bar, for decisive sporty car handling

with a comfortable passenger-car ride.

Great feeling. Driving a Mustang adds up to a statement of personal style. It feels great to you... it looks great to whoever's watching.

Discover Mustang for '73, at your Ford Dealer's.

FORD MUSTANG

FORD DIVISION *Ford*

All 1973 cars must meet Federal Emissions Standards before sale. See your Ford Dealer for details.

1973 Ford Mustang

Vintage 1973 Dinty Moore Beef Stew

8.2 Pitch Perfect: Slogans That Stood the Test of Time

In 1973, various slogans captured the spirit of the times, reflecting social and cultural movements, as well as advertising campaigns. Here are some of the most popular slogans from that year:

"**The Uncola**" - 7UP used this clever slogan to promote itself as a unique and refreshing alternative to traditional colas.

"Have it your way." (Burger King, 1973)
Before adapting the currently in use slogan "Be your way",
Burger King had been using another slogan for 40 years.
For 4 decades, Burger King has been associated with "Have
it your way".

"Because I'm Worth It" - L'Oréal introduced this slogan in 1973, emphasizing self-worth and promoting their beauty products.

"Probably the best lager in the world" (Carlsberg, 1973) Global brewer Carlsberg has used one of the most well-known advertising slogans in the world since 1973, until a rebranding move replaced it with the current slogan, "This calls for a Carlsberg".

Activity:
Historical Advertisement Scramble
~ Unscramble the slogans

Historical Advertisement Scramble - Unscramble the Slogans

Unscramble the slogans from historical advertisements in 1973. Here are the scrambled slogans:

"eTh Cnlucoa"..

"veHa ti oyu ywa."..

"eBeca,us Im' orWht I"..

We have heartfelt thank-you gifts for you

As a token of our appreciation for joining us on this historical journey through 1973, we've included a set of cards and stamps inspired by the year of 1973. These cards are your canvas to capture the essence of the past. We encourage you to use them as inspiration for creating your own unique cards, sharing your perspective on the historical moments we've explored in this book. Whether it's a holiday greeting or a simple hello to a loved one, these cards are your way to connect with the history we've uncovered together.

Happy creating!

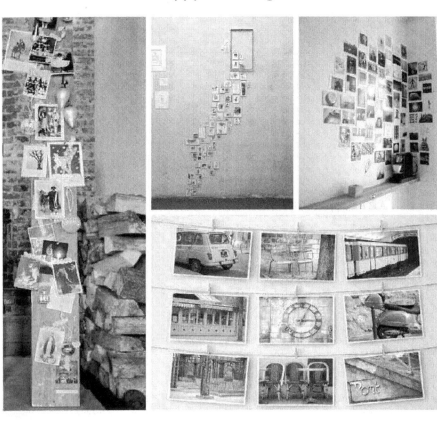

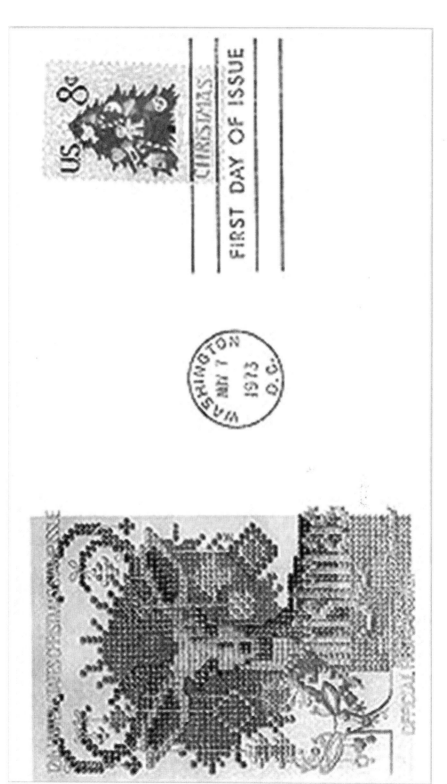

With best wishes for
Christmas
and
the New Year

Lilibet

Philip

1973

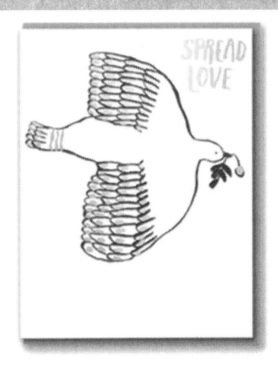

FIJI: 1973, QUEEN ELIZABETH II,
Christmas stamp

Activity Answers:

Chapter II:

Question 1:
Which classic film directed by George Lucas premiered in the United States in August 1973?

Answer: B) American Graffiti

Question 2:
Who won an Oscar for their role in "Paper Moon," becoming the youngest Oscar recipient ever at the age of nine?

Answer: A) Tatum O'Neal

Question 3:
Which crime drama television series, featuring Lieutenant Theo Kojak, aired from 1973 to 1978?

Answer: C) Kojak

Question 4:
In 1973, which actor won the Academy Award for Best Actor in a Leading Role for his iconic performance in "The Godfather"?

Answer: D) Marlon Brando

Question 5:
Who received the Best Actress award at the 1973 Academy Awards for her role in "Cabaret"?

Answer: C) Liza Minnelli

Question 6:
Which film earned Joel Grey an Oscar for Best Supporting Actor in 1973?

Answer: D) Cabaret

Question 7:
Eileen Heckart won the Best Supporting Actress award at the 1973 Academy Awards for her role in which movie?

Answer: C) Butterflies Are Free

Question 8:
How many episodes were there in "Star Trek: The Animated Series," which aired from 1973 to 1974?

Answer: C) 22 episodes

Question 9:
Which educational and entertaining TV show provided lessons on math, grammar, and civic topics through catchy songs?

Answer: C) Schoolhouse Rock!

Question 10:
In "Serpico," who played the role of the NYPD cop who dared to resist corruption?

Answer: A) Al Pacino

I hope you enjoyed the quiz and found it both entertaining and informative!

Chapter 3:
Strumming my pain with his fingers (one time, one time)
Singing my life with his words (two times, two times)
Killing me softly with his song
Killing me softly with his song
Telling my whole life with his words
Killing me softly with his song
I felt all flushed with fever, embarrassed by the crowd
I felt he'd found my letters and read each one out loud
I prayed that he would finish, but he just kept right on

Chapter 4:
Answers:
c) John Newcombe
c) 24
c) 18
c) Japan
c) O.J. Simpson
b) Oakland Athletics
c) London
a) Alex Higgins
b) 1972-73

Embracing 1973: A Grateful Farewell

Thank you for joining us on this journey through a year that holds a special place in our hearts. Whether you experienced 1973 firsthand or through the pages of this book, we hope it brought you moments of joy, nostalgia, and connection to a time that will forever shine brightly in our memories.

Share Your Thoughts and Help Us Preserve History

Your support and enthusiasm for this journey mean the world to us. We invite you to share your thoughts, leave a review, and keep the spirit of '73 alive. As we conclude our adventure, we look forward to more journeys through the annals of history together. Until then, farewell and thank you for the memories.

We would like to invite you to explore more of our fantastic world by scanning the QR code below. There you can easily get free ebooks from us and receive so many surprises.

TO DO LIST

- ◯ --
- ◯ --
- ◯ --
- ◯ --
- ◯ --
- ◯ --
- ◯ --
- ◯ --
- ◯ --
- ◯ --
- ◯ --
- ◯ --
- ◯ --
- ◯ --

well done!

To Do List

To Do List

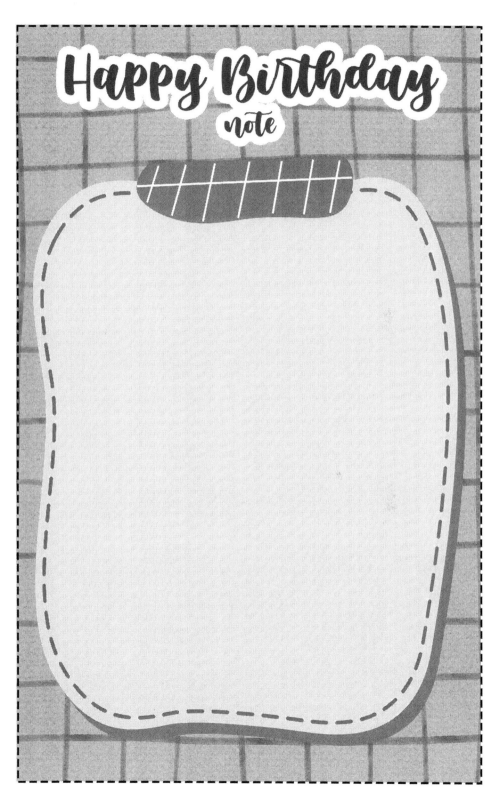

Happy Birthday
note

Happy Birthday

note

TO DO LIST

Name: _____ Day: _____ Month: _____

No	To Do List	Yes	No

TO DO LIST

Name: _____   Day: _____   Month: _____

No	To Do List	Yes	No

NOTE

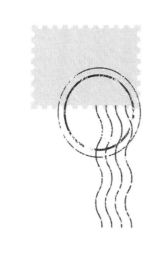

WISH YOU WERE HERE,
123 ANYWHERE ST., ANY CITY

HAPPY BIRTHDAY NOTE

TO DO LIST

Name: _____ Day: _____ Month: _____

No	To Do List	Yes	No

Remember This!
SPECTACLE ISLAND
Dorchester Point
Pulling Point
Powder Ho
Mill Pond

POSTCARD

To:

From:

Printed in Great Britain
by Amazon

32632091R00068